Would You Believe...

Vatican City
is a country?

and other metropolitan marvels

Richard Platt

OXFORD
UNIVERSITY PRESS

Contents

OXFORD
UNIVERSITY PRESS

Great Clarendon Street, Oxford OX2 6DP

Oxford University Press is a department of the University of Oxford. It furthers the University's objective of excellence in research, scholarship, and education by publishing worldwide in

Oxford New York

Auckland Cape Town Dar es Salaam Hong Kong Karachi Kuala Lumpur Madrid Melbourne Mexico City Nairobi New Delhi Shanghai Taipei Toronto

With offices in

Argentina Austria Brazil Chile Czech Republic France Greece Guatemala Hungary Italy Japan Poland Portugal Singapore South Korea Switzerland Thailand Turkey Ukraine Vietnam

Oxford is a registered trade mark of Oxford University Press in the UK and in certain other countries

Text copyright © Oxford University Press 2010

The moral rights of the author have been asserted

Database right Oxford University Press (maker)

First published 2010

British Library Cataloguing in Publication Data

Data available

ISBN 978-0-19-911970-7

1 3 5 7 9 10 8 6 4 2

Originated by Oxford University Press

Created by BOOKWORK Ltd

Printed in China by Imago

WARNING: *The practices in this book are for information only and should not be tried at home!*

Introduction

EXCITING, MAGNIFICENT, beautiful, historic – towns and cities can be all these things. They are wonderful places to live, work and play. But they have a darker side too, and can be crowded, noisy, polluted and threatening. Many towns and cities fit *both* these descriptions. Their citizens (the people who live there) learn to endure the hardships cheerfully so that they can enjoy the benefits.

Love them or hate them, you can't fail to be fascinated by cities and towns, for their history is the story of human life itself. Artists made their homes in cities, ruthless rulers built palaces there; greedy conquerors destroyed them.

But what is a town or city? How is it different from a village? Most of us would say "size", but there's more to it than that. In the past, everyone in a "village" farmed the surrounding countryside. Towns had homes for craftsmen and other workers who did not till the fields. Cities are the biggest towns, though in Britain a city always has a cathedral at its heart.

Would You Believe . . . ? Would You Believe . . . ?

Where, when, what and who?
Where did Mickey Mouse build a town? When did city traffic jams begin with chariots? Which country built its capital in the wrong place? What's beneath the city streets? Who taxed sewage collectors? If you want to know the answers, turn the page.

Before the City

FIXED, SOLID AND PERMANENT, towns and cities are the homes of people who want to stay put. However, the world's first people were a restless lot. They got their food by hunting and by gathering wild plants, so they had to move constantly to where there was food.

For them, city life would have been impossible. They would have quickly exhausted the food supplies. So they lived in temporary shelters that they could build quickly – and abandon when the food ran out.

▲ Hunting records
When modern humans first appeared, in Africa 200,000 years ago, they found food by hunting and gathering. The San people continued with this until recently. They recorded their hunts on the walls of the Stadsaal cave in South Africa where they sheltered.

▼ Cave dwellers
The earliest people were expert in making what they needed from stone, wood, bone and skin, but they could be wasteful and destructive. As long as they could always move on to fresh hunting grounds, there was no reason to conserve natural resources. City-dwellers had to be more careful.

Why did towns and cities begin? In the Neolithic (New Stone Age) period, people began to plant crops (food plants) and to rear animals. These farming methods made food more plentiful. That in turn meant that people could settle in one place.

But maybe towns came first?

It's possible that farming began *because* people built towns. Under the earliest cities, archaeologists have found bones of wild and farm animals. Did the people build comfortable homes then become farmers when they could no longer find enough food nearby?

Town or village? ▲
These remains are in Scotland's Neolithic village Skara Brae. It's not just size that made villages like this different from the towns that followed. Only farmers lived in villages. People who did not work in fields, such as traders and craftsmen lived in towns.

Would You Believe . . . ?

Farming folly
Farming was hard work, and farmers were hungrier and less healthy than their hunting and gathering cousins. So why did people continue to farm? Perhaps because they could sell crops at a good price to town dwellers, who used these to show off their wealth.

The word "civilization" comes from the Latin word for citizen – someone who lives in a city.

◀ **Neolithic daggers** ▲ ▶
The Neolithic people who first built towns were named for the fine stone tools and weapons that they made. Daggers were valuable for peaceful trade but had a violent use too. Town-builders used them to defend themselves from warrior neighbours.

▲ **Early farmers**
Without food plants, such as barley, there would be no cities. As the world's population grew, game (wild animals killed for food) became scarce. So 12,000 years ago, people in the Middle East began to plant seeds. By choosing the best, they could live off the fields.

You want to
Build it HERE?!

Timbuktu trade route ▲
Close to the Niger river, Africa, Timbuktu grew rich by controlling the route of gold and salt across the Sahara desert. Known only to Africans until 1828, Timbuktu fascinated Europeans. Its name became used for anything exciting or remote.

Frenchman **René Caillié** reached Timbuktu in 1828. He was expecting a golden city, but found only a dusty town.

The right spot ▼
British mariners called Sydney Harbour "the finest harbour in the world" when they sailed into it in 1788. Its deep water and shelter provided safe anchorages for 1,000 ships. The city has grown to be Australia's biggest.

SOME OF THE WORLD'S greatest cities are built in the oddest of places. For instance, Beijing, the capital of China, is in a remote north-east corner of the country. China's rulers built a palace there eight centuries ago to be close to their homeland further north, even though farmland nearby could never feed the growing city.

Most cities began for sensible reasons. Some controlled important trade routes. Many clung to cliffs or hilltops for protection. Their founders thought they would be impossible to capture there.

Sea towns
Cities such as Bristol grew up at the lowest point where it was possible to cross a river. In an age when ships were the fastest way to travel, a fine harbour always attracted settlers.

New town, new reasons

Times change. Straight sandy beaches make terrible harbours, but when sea-bathing became fashionable in the 18th century, they were perfect for resort towns. And today, San Francisco is one of the world's great cities, even though the gold that started it is just a memory.

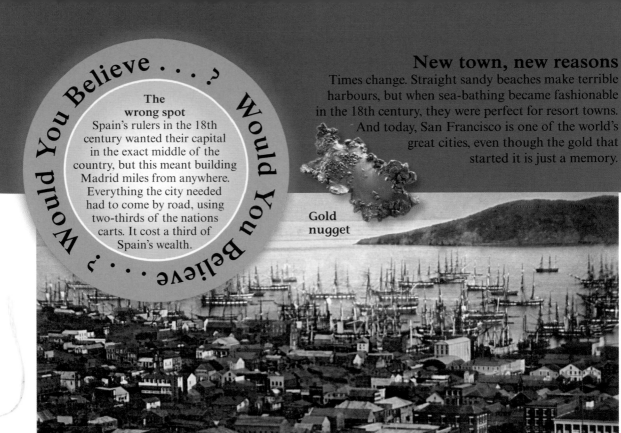

Gold nugget

Gold-rush city ▲

San Francisco was a sleepy hamlet with only 1,000 residents until 1848, when gold was found 170 km (100 miles) away. Within two years, its population was 25,000. The harbour, seen here in 1851, filled with abandoned ships as crews deserted to dig for gold.

Holding the hill ▶

When Roman soldiers invaded what is now France, more than 2,000 years ago, the native people retreated to their hilltop fort of Alesia. Under the leadership of Vercingetorix (right), they held off the Romans from their stronghold. The town fell only when the Romans surrounded it and cut off the food supplies.

Sydney Harbour bridge

7

The first Cities

A toy duck and a priest's statue found at Mohenjo-Daro

THE ANCIENT KINGDOM OF Sumer, in what is now southern Iraq, was an extraordinary place 5,000 years ago. For in this "land of cities", civilization began. The citizens of Babylon, Ur, Nineveh and many other towns were fed by crops grown in fertile fields between the Tigris and Euphrates rivers.

▲ Mohenjo-Daro
Home to up to 35,000 residents, Mohenjo-Daro in the Indus Valley was the biggest city in south Asia. Built 4,000 years ago of mud-brick, it had fortified towers, temples, public baths and grain stores.

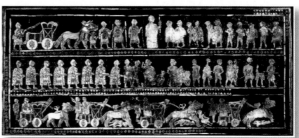

Ur mosaic ▲
A craftsman in a Sumerian city decorated this wooden box with scenes of life in war and, on the other side, peace. Called the Standard (flag) of Ur, its shell and blue-stone patterns include chariots and men in armoured cloaks with spears.

By 2000 BCE, nine out of every ten people lived in towns in the land of Sumer. Cities were growing and thriving to the south too, in Egypt, and further east in the Indus Valley (now Pakistan).

◀ Neolithic mod-cons
Built 9,500 years ago, Catal Huyuk in Turkey was a farming village. Though all its residents worked in fields, it was like the first cities that grew up centuries later. Ladders from a maze of plastered homes led to flat roofs that acted as streets.

Sumerian city-dwellers ate a lot of onions: their word for garden, *ki-sum-ma*, translates as "onion growing land"

These early cities had one thing in common: writing. Driven by the needs of their traders and priests, the people pressed words into soft mud or painted them on paper, leaving vivid pictures of their lives.

Nothing changes

Early cities were crowded, dirty and noisy – just like today's cities. They were modern in other ways too. Mohenjo-Daro in the Indus Valley had sewers and running water. To keep order in Babylon, a code of laws punished crimes, such as burglary, which still make urban life miserable.

Memphis ▶
Little remains of Memphis in the Nile Valley except this sphinx (cat/human figure) and a few ruins. But 4,500 years ago, Memphis was different. It was the capital of Lower (north) Egypt and the world's largest city, with 30,000 citizens. But as other cities grew important, its building stone was plundered.

Would You Believe . . . ?

City code
Babylon's ruler Hammurabi made laws to control the city: housebreakers were executed and buried at the crime scene; anyone stealing from a burning house was pushed into the flames; tavern-keepers overcharging for their beer were thrown in the river.

AROUND THE WARM waters of the Mediterranean Sea, some of the greatest cities of the ancient world flourished. Knossos, Athens, Alexandria and Troy all prospered, but for true power and glory – and crowding and squalor – no city compared with the city of Rome.

Home to 800,000 people in 180 CE, Rome had many of the advantages of a modern city. There was ample fresh water and cheap public baths, the streets were paved, there were grand public buildings and shops sold luxury goods brought from afar.

Troy ▶
In ancient legends, Troy was a glittering city in what is now Turkey, and its people rivalled the Greeks for power. Archaeologists have found nine Troys, built one on top of another. These coins, from the most recent city, are about 2,200 years old. The lowest, oldest city dates from 2,500 years earlier.

The bath house

In Rome, a soak in a hot pool cost no more than the city's smallest coin. As the Romans conquered Europe, they built baths in the new cities that they created. All followed the same pattern, with lashings of luxurious hot water and underfloor central heating – a popular Roman invention.

Decline and fall

Despite their grandeur, all these magnificent Mediterranean cities fell into ruins. Most were capitals of wealthy empires. They thrived as the empires expanded, but when imperial power grew weaker and failed, the cities fell. Some disappeared: even Troy's location was forgotten.

Athens was grand but filthy: on its sprawling, stinking rubbish dumps citizens left unwanted babies to die

● ●

▲ The baths at Bath
So good, they named the city after them, the famous Roman baths at England's city of Bath are still fed from hot underground springs.

▼ Rome
The people of Rome were chariot-racing fans, and there was enough space at the stadium, the *Circus Maximus*, for every free citizen. Horses pulled chariots around a course some 600 m (1,970 ft) long. Booths sold spectators food, drink or fortune telling.

Knossos ▲
In the middle of the Greek island of Crete, Knossos was the centre of Minoan civilization that grew up around 4,700 years ago. The palace at the city's heart had more than 1,300 rooms, ranging from humble grain and olive oil stores to vast and magnificent throne halls. This "Lily Prince" mural decorated its walls.

▲ Locker room
The baths at Pompeii, Italy, were perfectly preserved when a volcano covered the city in ash in 44 CE. This view shows the *apodyterium*, the changing room. Bathers stripped here, leaving a slave to guard their belongings, before going on to a cold plunge pool, then warm and hot baths.

11

Medieval Towns and Cities

The cutpurse ▲
Crowds in towns made thieves' work easy. This painting shows a cutpurse stealing from someone distracted by a conjuring trick. People carried their belongings in purses on their belts. Clothes didn't have pockets until the 16th century.

WHEN ROMAN CIVILIZATION collapsed in the 5th century CE, many benefits of city life disappeared too. In the Middle Ages – and the 1,000 or so years that followed – European cities became unpleasant places to live, especially for the poor. Many cities grew largely unplanned within a surrounding wall. Without space to expand, they were noisy, crowded, dirty, smelly and unhealthy.

Would You Believe . . . ?

Filthy floors
Medieval cities were filthy indoors and out. 15th-century Dutch writer Erasmus complained of the "strew" – a layer of rushes that carpeted London floors. Beneath it lay "ancient ... beer, grease, fish bones, spittle, excrement of dogs and cats and everything else that's nasty."

Homes and trade ▲
Houses, shops and industry crowded together in medieval towns, making life unpleasant for residents. Londoners complained that armour makers did their hammering at night, after idly drinking all day, and that their furnaces sprayed sparks that started fires.

Why live in a town? Craftsmen came to set up workshops and merchants came to find customers. Others wanted to leave the countryside where they were virtually slaves. A saying went, "Town air makes men free."

Wealth and comfort
Rich citizens lived comfortably. Servants kept their spacious houses clean, and in the streets they travelled above the muck, on horseback or in smart carriages. However, when disease struck the city, wealth was no protection. The rich died just like the poor.

▼ Living in comfort

People from wealthy, powerful families did not have to suffer the misery that others in medieval cities endured. In this 15th-century picture, the French Duc de Berry (in blue on right) hosts a lavish New Year's feast.

◀ Although it was no cure for the plague, 14th-century monks queued for a priest's blessing.

Plague and pestilence ▲

Poor hygiene and cramped living conditions in cities meant that disease spread more rapidly than in the countryside. When a plague swept across Europe in the 14th century, one-third of city people died. Some country areas escaped infection.

● ● ● ● ● ● ● ● ● ● ● ● ● ● ● ● ●

Medieval cities controlled the height of street dunghills – they made the houses they leaned against damp!

▼ Flushed down the river

Cities on rivers often used them to wash away foul waste, such as the guts from slaughtered animals. However, some used rivers more carefully. The German city of Ulm (below) used the Danube in its 11 bath-houses.

Keeping out Strangers

▲ Great Zimbabwe
Walls enclosed communities throughout Africa. South of the Sahara desert, the most famous are Zimbabwe's. Spread across the country named after it, Zimbabwe was so grand that white explorers could not believe that Africans built them.

▼ Forbidden city
At the heart of Beijing, the Forbidden City was the palace of China's emperor. Built in the 15th century, the palace was protected by huge walls made mostly of earth because stone was scarce.

SINCE THE VERY EARLIEST cities began to rise on the plains of Sumer thousands of years ago, thick walls were built to encircle and protect their inhabitants. As an official of one German city summed it up in 1399: "What has a wall around it, that we call a city."

It wasn't just European people who longed for the security that high, strong walls could bring. Stone and mud ramparts protected towns and cities as far apart as eastern Asia and southern Africa.

Break through
Walls were an effective defence until the 15th century. Then, cannons brought from China gave attacking armies a quick way to blast an entrance. A few cities built new walls thick enough to withstand cannon attack, but these took up as much space as the town within.

▼ Carcassonne
The Romans were the first to protect this city in southern France with walls, but most of the ramparts and towers date from the Middle Ages. Restored in the mid 19th century, Carcassonne's walls are as perfect as when they were first built.

14

In ancient China, walls and cities were the same, and in Chinese writing they share the same character – 城

Down with walls!

Even when walls were effective, not everybody liked them. They were costly and stopped cities expanding. When they were no longer needed for defence, they were destroyed. But where a wall has disappeared, traces often remain in road names in the city.

◀ **Montereggioni**
The strong walls of this town in Tuscany, Italy, provided little protection when the town was attacked in 1554. Its commanding officer surrendered after just a day, claiming that the town's well had been destroyed. The townspeople accused him of being a traitor, in the pay of the enemy.

Would You Believe . . . ? Would You Believe . . . ? Would You Believe

Ker-twang!
Walls couldn't always protect a city's inhabitants. When the Christian city of Caffa (now Feodosiya, Ukraine) was besieged in 1347, Muslim attackers used catapults to hurl rotting corpses over the walls. This primitive form of biological warfare helped spread the Black Death all over Europe.

Constantinople ▶
The port of Constantinople, now Istanbul in Turkey, was surrounded by elaborate walls from Roman times. They protected the city from attacks by both sea and land and turned away enemies for 600 years. But in 1453, the city fell to an Ottoman army equipped with cannons.

Floating Towns

WHEN SPANISH SOLDIERS marched into the heart of Mexico in 1519, an astonishing sight greeted them. In the middle of a vast lake floated a fairy-tale city. Much bigger than anything in Spain, its brilliant white city walls shone in the sun like jewels.

Tenochtitlan (now Mexico City) was not *actually* afloat. It was built on an island. Causeways (raised roads) linked it to the shore. Countless canoes ferried supplies to it.

Tenochtitlan's lake was a rich source of food; besides fish and game, residents ate algae and the eggs of water insects

Tenochtitlan ▲
Tenochtitlan had a dark secret: its Aztec rulers carried out grisly human sacrifices on pyramids in its centre. Appalled, and greedy for its golden treasures, the Spanish captured the city – then totally destroyed it.

Male, Maldives ▲
You can walk around Male, the capital of the Maldives, in an hour, yet one-third of the Maldives' people live here. The island setting causes problems. Water pumped from below ground needs salt removing before it's fit to drink, and rubbish has to be dumped in the sea nearby.

Safe islands
In the past, islands made great locations for cities. The surrounding water had all the advantages of a defensive moat, a sewer and a productive farm. And at a time when boats and ships were the fastest transport, the sea was like a modern highway.

Palm Islands, Dubai ▶
On the shore of the Arabian desert, Dubai has created three island towns shaped like palm trees. Luxurious homes line their "fronds", but they are not perfect. In summer, air conditioning can cost as much as rent elsewhere in the city.

Rare cities

Mexico's lake dried up long ago, but you can still visit enchanting island cities, such as Venice in Italy. Newer floating cities are rare. Towns no longer need watery defences, and an island setting limits growth and makes it costly to bring in supplies.

Venice ▼
Six centuries ago, the island city of Venice was one of the great sea powers. Its ships controlled trade with the Arab world and the city was the richest in Europe. Today, it is tourists that support Venice, but the city is still as astonishing and spectacular as it was centuries ago, rising out of its ocean lagoon like an incredible movie fantasy.

Would You Believe . . . ?

Rich Venice
Venice is still one of the world's most beautiful and picturesque cities. Its richness can be too much for some visitors. American writer Truman Capote said in 1961 that experiencing Venice was "like eating an entire box of chocolate liqueurs in one go".

Extreme Cities

IMAGINE LIVING WHERE rain never falls, or where it's so cold that water thrown up in the air tinkles back down as ice. Imagine living so high up a mountain that you have to gasp for breath because there is so little air. People have built cities in places that really are as extreme as this – and still live there.

Life in some extreme towns is hardly comfortable. Longyearbyen in Norway, for example, is so far north that the sun doesn't rise from October to February, but coal mining provides work and wealth.

Cold: Archangelsk ▲
In north Russia, the port of Archangelsk is home to 400,000 shivering people. In winter, it can be so cold that wearing spectacles outside is unwise because they freeze to your face. In the Middle Ages, the city was Russia's main port – though outside the short summer, sea ice locked ships in the harbour.

▼ Dry: Arica
The barren Atacama Desert behind the port of Arica in Chile is so dry that even the dead don't decay in the salty sand – they just slowly turn to wizened mummies. In 1868, an earthquake and tsunami destroyed the city (below), but today, in spite of the conditions, about 200,000 people live there.

During a drought in the high, remote city of Potosí, a jug of water once sold for the equivalent of six weeks' wages

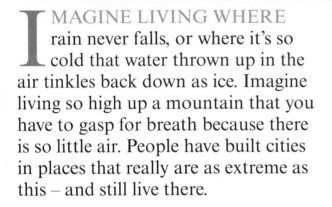

...inhabited city is Potosí in Bolivia, at 4000 m (13,000 ft). The air is thin, but it became rich overnight in 1545. Silver was discovered here, and miners swelled the population to 200,000.

Danger makes some of the greatest cities extreme. Earthquakes could destroy Los Angeles tomorrow, and Naples in Italy sits under a volcano. The people know they risk disaster, but this doesn't drive them away.

Remote: Iquitos ▶

Iquitos in Peru is the hardest city to get to. Deep in the rainforest, it cannot be reached by road, and visitors have to arrive by boat up the Amazon river or by float plane. The city's Belén district (right) floods annually, so houses stand on floats and local products are traded in the floating market.

Would You Believe . . . ? Would You Believe ? Would You Believe

Wet, wet, wet!
The world's wettest town is Cherrapunji in India. In July 1861, nearly 10 m (30 ft) of rain fell here! Though Cherrapunji is soaked in the monsoon (storm) season, it has a drought in mid winter, and residents have to fetch water from far away.

Surprising
Cities

WAKING UP SURROUNDED BY dead bodies sounds like a nightmare, but for the million residents of Cairo's City of the Dead, it happens each morning. The Egyptian capital's poor moved to the cemetery when rents soared too high for them. Now the graveyard homes have plumbing and electricity.

One ancient town in Cappadocia, Turkey, lies completely underground. Some modern cities have copied it: Toronto and Montreal in Canada both have vast networks of streets buried out of reach of the winter.

Is it a city ... or a nation?
National boundaries cut some cities in two or enclose them completely. Vatican City is a city-within-a-city. The headquarters of the Catholic Church, it lies inside Italy's capital, Rome, and is the only city in the world that's also a country.

Petra ▶
"A rose-red city half as old as time", Petra is a remarkable complex of buildings cut from the rock in Jordan. Occupied since 10,000 BCE, the city grew rich by controlling a trade route. Its Nabataean people supplied their desert city with water by trapping rare torrential rains and tapping underground springs.

Would You Believe . . . ? Would You Believe . . . ?

Split town
In an 18th-century mapping blunder, surveyors drew the USA-Canada border through a town. Now with two names, Derby Line (Vermont) and Rock Island (Quebec) straddle the border. Some homes have their kitchen in one country and their dining room in the other.

◀ Cappadocia
The people of Turkey's Cappadocia region began tunnelling out underground cities more than 2,500 years ago. The volcanic rock of the region is soft to dig out but hardens when the air gets to it, so the excavated rooms are well supported.

◄ Vatican City
A palace, a city, a country – Vatican City is all of these. Ruled by the Pope, it's home to about 800 people. The size of only 61 soccer pitches, the city-state has its own police force and also the world's shortest railway, running just 14 m (46 ft).

Because it is also a nation, Vatican City is the only city that has its own passports

New populations
Some of these surprising cities attract visitors long after they have been abandoned by their residents. Tourists flock to see Jordan's extraordinary and beautiful rock-cut city of Petra and the houses that cling like swallows' nests to one of Colorado's cliffs.

▲ Mesa Verde
Wedged under an overhanging rock in Colorado, USA, Mesa Verde is an extraordinary cliff town. The Anasazi people built it around 1150 CE, creating multi-level homes, including the Cliff Palace shown here. By careful use of their scarce water supplies, they were able to grow crops on the table-like hilltop above their homes.

A quiet neighbourhood ▶
Nearly one-third of Cairo's 16 million people live in refurbished tombs in a cemetery. Some of them are paid to guard the tombs. Others move here to be close to the spirits of lost ancestors, but most have nowhere else to live. To some Egyptians, there's nothing sinister about having the dead for neighbours.

Planning for People

W HO WOULD WANT TO LIVE on a factory estate? Or walk past dung on their way home? Today, this doesn't happen. Planning rules keep houses, factories, offices and shops apart. It wasn't like this in the past. People often had waste-tips on their doorsteps.

Greek streets ▲
The ancient city of Miletus (now in Turkey) was the first grid city. Architect Hippodamus designed it with blocks of buildings reserved for different purposes. Today, visitors can still see the street outlines around this temple.

City planning really began in Greece in the 5th century BCE. There, architect Hippodamus planned streets on a grid, separating each kind of building on different blocks.

◄ Egyptian temple towns
Clustered close to the Nile river, the cities of ancient Egypt were planned by the country's priests. Temples followed patterns of ever-smaller squares. This forest of huge columns once held up a temple roof at Karnak, Luxor.

New York grid city ▼
New York is the most famous grid city in the world. The first settlers on Manhattan Island, now a borough in the city, started building at the island's most southern tip and moved northwards. Streets followed animal tracks until 1811, then a policeman, a lawyer and a surveyor devised a rigid grid plan for the north part of the island to speed up its development.

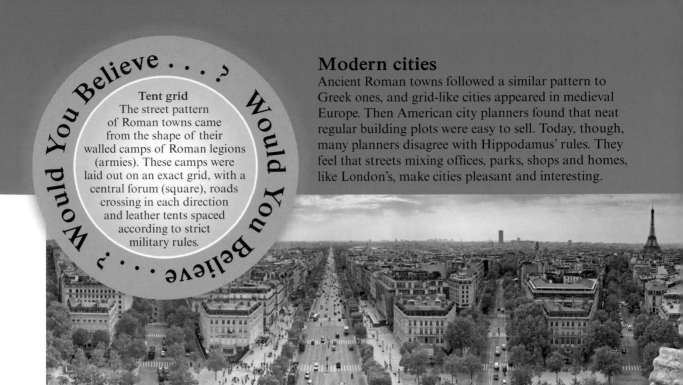

Would You Believe . . . ? **Would You Believe . . . ?**

Tent grid
The street pattern of Roman towns came from the shape of their walled camps of Roman legions (armies). These camps were laid out on an exact grid, with a central forum (square), roads crossing in each direction and leather tents spaced according to strict military rules.

Modern cities

Ancient Roman towns followed a similar pattern to Greek ones, and grid-like cities appeared in medieval Europe. Then American city planners found that neat regular building plots were easy to sell. Today, though, many planners disagree with Hippodamus' rules. They feel that streets mixing offices, parks, shops and homes, like London's, make cities pleasant and interesting.

Straight, parallel streets are not always best: San Francisco's rigid grid sends streets straight up incredibly steep hills.

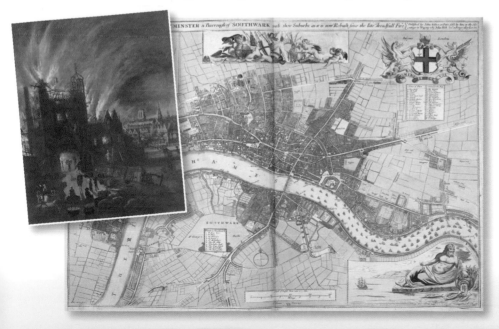

Revolting Parisians ▲
When revolution rocked France at the end of the 18th century, the rebellious Parisians easily closed off the capital's narrow streets with barricades. When Georges Haussmann rebuilt the city centre half a century later, he planned it with straight boulevards (streets) that were too wide to block.

◀ Missed opportunity
When fire destroyed London in 1666, there was a chance to build a beautiful new city. Several grand grid-plans were proposed, but after a lot of bickering, the city was rebuilt along the same rambling streets the fire had destroyed. This map, made in 1680, shows what the rebuilt London looked like.

Starting from Scratch

WHAT MAKES A PERFECT CITY? Politicians, tycoons and businesses often think they know. The towns and cities they built from the 19th century onwards were planned to be spacious, airy, green and beautiful. Some succeeded: Bournville, built by chocolate millionaire George Cadbury, was called "the nicest place in Britain".

▲ Dream or nightmare?
Architect Oscar Niemeyer and planner Lucio Costa designed a new capital for Brazil in the 1950s. Called Brasilia, it grew in four years in the middle of the country. Its buildings brought worldwide praise, but the city grew too quickly. Planned for 500,000, Brasilia now has 2.2 million residents.

Perfection doesn't come easy. Real cities are never as neat or as clean as architects' plans. Brazil's capital, for example, was a victim of its own success. Millions of poor people moved there, building slums that spoiled the views.

Would You Believe . . . ? Would You Believe . . . ?

Paintwork police state
To make sure that people in Celebration (see p. 25) don't paint their houses clashing colours, the town has good-taste police. Called *Celebration Home Enhancement*, they tour the streets in golf buggies checking not only exterior paint but curtains and wallpaper too.

◄ Garden cities
Dirt, crime and disease in 19th-century cities inspired British writer Ebeneezer Howard to demand better homes for working people. The "garden cities" he suggested combined the advantages of town and country. They were planned from scratch, surrounded by farmland and limited in size. Letchworth (left) was one of the first.

Bush Capital ▶
The plan of Australia's capital city Canberra was decided by a competition in 1912. The winning architects were fans of the garden city movement and incorporated many green areas, earning Canberra the nickname "Bush Capital".

Perfectly ... boring?

Planners of the newest "model towns" have learned a lesson. Strict rules ensure that there's "... a lemonade seller, not a mugging, on every street corner". They're safe and they're clean – but not everyone would choose to live in one.

Shacks built by the poor near Brasilia were removed and dumped far away

▲ **Soap star homes**
When a British soap manufacturer built a town for his workers in 1899, he named it Port Sunlight after his best-selling product. None of the 800 houses were alike and the workers all paid low rents.

◀ **Planning paradise**
Old buildings get in the way of architects' bold visions, so dream towns usually rise in open country. When construction of the resort of Cancun, Mexico, began in 1970, just three coconut farmers lived on the island.

▲ **Mickey Mouse town**
The Disney corporation built Celebration, Florida, as the perfect American town. Close to Disney's theme-park, its pretty houses might have come from a movie themselves. And at Christmas, foam "snow" falls from streetlights.

High-rise City

UNTIL 1890, FEW offices were more than five storeys tall – engineers did not know how to protect taller structures from fire or collapse and when stairs were the only way up, higher floors were impossible to rent. The construction of skyscrapers began when high land prices forced developers to build up, not out, squeezing more offices on to smaller plots.

● ● ● ● ● ● ● ● ● ● ● ●

Engineering breakthroughs made it possible to build tall. Skyscrapers could not exist until there were strong steel frames to hold them up, powerful pumps to raise drinking water, lifts to carry residents to the top and new materials to stop fires.

Manhattan monkey business ▶
When a giant gorilla prowled New York in the 1933 movie *King Kong*, he fled to the highest place he could find: one of the city's skyscrapers. These tall buildings crowded Manhattan even then, and the famous skyline forms the backdrop to this movie poster.

Tall buildings were called cloud-supporters, sky-batterers, sky-sweepers and cloud-busters, but only skyscrapers stuck

It will never stay up!
Many thought gales would topple early skyscrapers, so when storms struck New York's 13-floor Tower Building in 1888, architect Bradford Gilbert climbed to the top to show it was safe. The structure didn't budge – but he was almost blown off into the crowd below.

▼ Streets in the sky
Built in 1952, flats in the Unité d'Habitation (housing unit) in Marseille, France, were some of the first high-rise homes. French architect Le Corbusier provided "streets" every three floors, which included shops, a gym and a theatre.

Mud-brick marvels ▶
Five centuries ago, people built tower houses of up to 11 storeys high in the city of Shibam in Yemen. Their height protected the residents from raiders. The towers are built from mud-bricks, which need regular renewal.

◀ Petronas Towers
At 452 m (1,483 ft) these double skyscrapers in Kuala Lumpur, Malaysia, take the record for the world's highest twin buildings. But not everyone loves them. As with most tall towers, their construction used scarce resources, they are greedy for energy and water and they tangle city traffic.

Growing skyscrapers ▲
Chicago's 10-storey Home Insurance Building (above left) of 1885 was the first skyscraper. Later skyscrapers were much taller. The 1931 Empire State Building in New York (above centre) stood 381 m (1,250 ft) high. It was the world's tallest building for more than 40 years. Today, Dubai's Burj Dubai (above right) holds that record. It will be a staggering 818 m (2,684 ft) high when complete.

Suburban Bliss

A S MEDIEVAL TOWNS grew more crowded, citizens who yearned for space built houses outside the walls – and created suburbs. They took a risk that suburban home owners no longer face: the suburbs were the first places to be trashed and burned when hostile neighbours attacked a city.

The growth of railways in the late 19th century spread suburbs further. Developers built houses within walking distance of stations strung out along the track. Suburb dwellers travelled daily to work in the city.

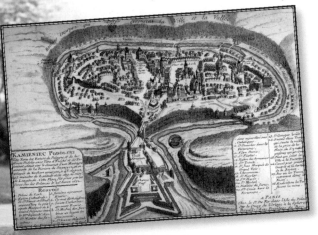

Castle, wall and suburb ▲
In this 1691 view of the city of Kamianets-Podilskyi, Ukraine, the castle, at the bottom, is walled for defence. The Smotrych river surrounds and protects the city, but on the other side of the river scattered houses mark the beginnings of the city's suburb. Today it is many times the size of the old town.

▲ Dream home
Mid-20th-century families fled from cities in search of clean air and safe neighbourhoods. Suburbs really did provide these: cul-de-sacs (dead-end roads) cut down speeding traffic, and children could walk to school together, leaving parents with freedom at home.

Permitted suburb ▶
High walls closed off the imperial city of Beijing to ordinary Chinese people living in the suburbs (shown here in 1830). Officials and nobles could enter but were excluded from the Forbidden City, the emperor's palace at the capital's centre.

In Chaucer's *Canterbury Tales* (1386), the Canon's Yeoman lives "in the suburbs of a towne"

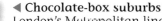

Motor cars changed suburbs in the 1930s. They began to sprawl thinly across huge areas. Gardens were bigger, but owners had to drive everywhere. Malls with vast car parks replaced local shops.

Smart or just smug?
Many city dwellers scorn suburbs. They sneer at the houses as identical boxes for people with matching minds. Yet suburbanites don't care. They have spacious homes on leafy streets, close to the city yet beyond its dangers.

◀ Chocolate-box suburbs
London's Metropolitan line advertised suburbs that sprung up along it in the 20th century as "Metro-Land". Poet John Betjeman said residents included "a city clerk turned countryman again, and linked to the metropolis by trains".

▲ Motor suburbs
Residents pay extra for houses on suburban streets because busy roads bypass them. However, today, accident statistics suggest that cul-de-sacs are not as safe as people think: children play on the quiet drives and risk being reversed over by suburban motorists.

IF YOU WANT A CITY, AND you want it fast, forget bricks and mortar – they are far too slow, too heavy and too expensive. Fortunately, there are much quicker ways of constructing temporary housing, and cheaper materials too. The most popular is canvas.

▲ **Siege town**
In ancient warfare, soldiers lived in a tent town during a siege (when they attacked a walled city by surrounding it). Here, an army led by Babylonian king Nebuchadnezzar II camps out around Jerusalem in 587 BCE.

◀ **Land grab**
In April 1889, the US State of Oklahoma gave away land from which it had driven the Native Americans. 10,000 settlers claimed a spot with a tent. Ten years later, Oklahoma City stood on this land.

▲ **Racing to build**
Which town gets built anew every four years and lasts just two weeks? The answer is the "village" where the Olympic athletes live while they compete. Host cities, such as Beijing (above), sell the homes after the games.

Armies have always been expert at making tent cities. Soldiers must move fast, and they need shelter that they can carry on their backs. Tents have done the job since warfare itself began, though they don't keep out arrows or bullets.

Komonik 12. Sammia Gar...
...illian tent 50 m... can su...
...had a tiled floor that was...
carried round in sections.

All mod cons

Just because your home blows in the wind, you don't have to "rough it". In extreme climates, some tents feel like regular buildings to the people inside. They have hot showers, floors, insulation and proper kitchens. Those at the Hajj in Saudi Arabia (below) even have air-conditioning.

Would You Believe . . . ?

A town in a month

In 1892, a chemical company in the USA built a real town in a month to house their workers in Wyoming. After 30 days, 200 families moved into Johnstown. The company even provided a school for their kids, complete with a teacher and books!

▲ Fans under canvas

Music lovers build their own canvas city at festivals such as Glastonbury in the UK. Around 140,000 camp out, and the site would soon become a severe health hazard without proper planning. Organisers provide clean water, lavatories and a few showers, but many fans still leave completely caked in mud.

Pilgrims' city ▼

Muslims have a duty to make a Hajj (holy journey) to Mecca, Saudi Arabia, once in their lives. Each year, nearly 3 million people make this journey and stay in a gigantic temporary city of 40,000 tents. Fires killed 340 people there in 1997, so the tents are now made of flameproof material.

Ancient city suppliers

As towns grew bigger, citizens faced long walks to resources, such as wells and farms, so they needed services. Twenty-seven centuries ago, aqueducts (water channels) kept Roman taps running.

Servicing the City

CITIES NEVER SLEEP, EVEN AT the darkest hours. Without 24/7 attention, they would soon become dangerous and unpleasant places to live. So small armies of people work to maintain and clean, and supply everything citizens need.

The effort involved in maintaining a city is mostly invisible. Those who do vital jobs are not around when we are. We notice them only when things go wrong and taps or switches don't work.

◀ **Serving thirsty Romans**
Soaring nearly 50 m (165 ft) above a French valley, the Pont du Gard bridge carries an aqueduct that brought water to the Roman city of Nîmes from springs 50 km (30 miles) away. Built in the first century CE, the aqueduct delivered enough water daily for 176,000 baths.

Would You Believe . . . ?

Filthy money
In ancient Rome, urine from lavatories was sold to launderers as a detergent. When emperor Vespasian taxed this service, his son Titus said that taxing urine was disgusting because it stank. Vespasian held up a gold coin and told Titus not to complain because the gold didn't stink!

In 100 CE, Rome supplied each citizen with ten times as much water as the people of London enjoyed in 1910

Gardez l'eau ▶
European plumbing in the 18th century was primitive, so residents emptied their chamber pots into the street from their windows. It was polite to shout *"gardez l'eau"* (beware of the water) before emptying a pot, to give those below a chance to avoid a drenching.

▲ Damping down the dust
The changing urban scene has made some services unnecessary. Before streets were paved, they turned to dust in summer. Water carts like this solved the problem in the 19th century, damping down the streets on dry days.

Night market ▲
Fresh food traders in all the world's cities use the night hours to buy from wholesale markets goods that they will sell the following day. Some markets, such as this one in Taiwan's capital, Taipei, also open at night to sell goods to the public.

◀ City sweeper
Before motor vehicles replaced horse transport, city streets had to be swept constantly or heaps of steaming, stinking horse dung would soon have blocked them. Today, sweepers still do a very important health job: rats, which spread disease, feast on tasty morsels they find in discarded litter.

▲ Modern mechanical sweeper

33

Beneath the City Streets

A vast web of buried copper cables carries power to city homes and offices.

WHAT'S UNDER YOUR FEET in the city? Sewage, water and gas pipes are easy things to guess. You might also think of electricity, phone and data cables. But what about hidden rivers, huge graveyards and even forgotten streets? Dig a very deep hole and you could find any of these things beneath your feet in a city.

Cities hide a lot of unexpected stuff because they once grew without planning. Each generation piled new buildings and roads on top of what had gone before. People soon forget what they bury.

▲ Close ghosts
When the merchants of Edinburgh, Scotland, needed a market in 1750, there was no empty land, so they built it on top of seven levels of closes (narrow streets) where people had been living and working. Recently unearthed, the buried streets around Mary King's Close are rumoured to be haunted.

◄ Forgotten river
Rivers are a nuisance in cities because heavy rain makes them flood and residents throw in rubbish, blocking them. So city authorities usually cover over these annoying water-courses. With buildings above them, they are soon forgotten. London alone has more than ten lost rivers. This brick tunnel carries the Fleet. Once you could row up it; now it's remembered only in the name of Fleet Street.

Modern underground services

Today, pipes and cables are so tangled that utility companies' diggers risk damaging what's already there. To help workers spot vital services, they are colour coded. In Britain, gas pipes are yellow and water pipes blue. Where possible, new services follow old routes: telecoms fibres in London run in pressure pipes abandoned years ago.

◄ Stinky but essential
City dwellers like to "flush and forget", but sewage doesn't just vanish. To carry away human waste safely, cities have networks of pipes and tunnels leading to treatment plants. Prague's century-old sewers, shown here, include 350 km (220 miles) of tunnels.

Cities get buried in building materials and dirt: every ten days the ground rises by the thickness of a page of a book

Rest in peace ▼
When graveyards got crowded, some cities freed up space by moving older skeletons into tunnels, called catacombs. In Paris, seven million skeletons are stored in 300 km (200 miles) of tunnels that were first dug as quarries. This skull is from the catacombs of Palermo, Italy.

Problem
Cities

CITIES HAVE A DARK SIDE. They can be messy, noisy and dangerous. Crime thrives in streets where no one knows who their neighbour is. And it's the success of cities that causes these problems. There just isn't enough room for all the people who flock to them seeking work and opportunity.

City problems began long ago: even in ancient Sumer, street noise woke sleepers. But today, half the world lives in cities so more suffer these drawbacks.

◄ The big smoke
Chinese cities burn coal to generate electricity. The result is choking smog which kills about 6,500 people every year in Shanghai (left). Air pollution is even worse in other Chinese cities.

◄ Homeless and hungry
High costs make city housing a luxury that many cannot afford. People who have to sleep on the streets suffer more from mental illness and are more likely to depend on drugs or alcohol than those with somewhere to live. Once treated as criminals, the homeless are now more likely to get some help – though often from charities not their city councils.

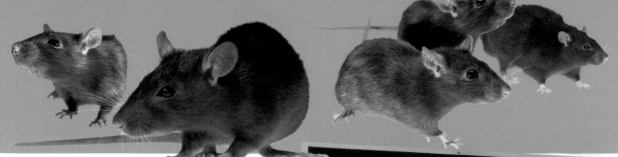

▲ Ancient companions

According to urban legends, you are never more than 3 m (10 ft) away from a rat in the city. Rats breed quickly, spread disease and raid bin bags for food.

● ● ● ● ● ● ● ● ● ● ● ● ●

Tackling urban problems is tough, but not impossible. Sometimes small changes help a lot. Keeping the most polluting vehicles out of city centres improves the air quality, and routing traffic down side streets can cut crime there, because burglars prefer quiet neighbourhoods.

Organised crime ▶

Criminals can make big profits in cities – as long as nobody bothers them. Gangster Al "Scarface" Capone grew rich in 1920s Chicago by smuggling alcohol, which was banned at the time. He even bribed the city's mayor to ignore his gang's activities. In the 1932 film *Scarface*, Capone was fictionalised as "Antonio 'Tony' Camonte" (played by Paul Muni).

◀ Mafia town

In the Italian city of Naples, crime gangs called the Camorra use threats and murder to influence local politics. Rubbish piles up in the streets whenever the council threatens to reform rubbish collection, which gangs control.

Slums, Ghettos
and Shanty Towns

MAKING A "HOUSE" FROM cardboard boxes is a favourite way for kids everywhere to play. But for millions of families, it's no game: they really do live in houses built from rubbish or in fragile shacks. Altogether, one-sixth of the world's homes are in slums – bad neighbourhoods without any facilities such as electricity, running water and sewers.

▼ **Slum or factory?**
Called *bastis* (settlements) locally, the slums of Kolkata (Calcutta), India, look run-down, but their residents make most of the shoes and clothes manufactured in the city. Developers long to clear the one in Rajabazar (below), just because it borders a smart neighbourhood.

Would You Believe . . . ? Would You Believe . . . ?

Rookery nook
London's 18th-century Rookeries rivalled modern-day slums. One house in four sold illegal alcohol, and one room could be a home for up to 20 people. Cellars were so damp that one family had to cross theirs in a boat made from a barrel.

◄ **First ghetto**
These Jewish signs are in Venice's Ghetto, the small area of the Italian city where Jews were forced to live from 1516. Since then, "ghetto" has come to mean a city region packed with people of one race or background.

Squatter city

Not all of the informal housing surrounding busy cities is as run-down as its "slum" label suggests. Shanty towns are just illegal or squatter settlements. Determined residents sometimes succeed in getting connected to the services they need and making their new homes official.

Most slums surround cities. Poverty in the countryside drives people to them. Some cities would be empty if their slum dwellers left tomorrow: for example, more than half of the people in Mumbai, India, live in slums.

Out of sight, out of mind

City councils regularly "clear" slums, driving people into ever more crowded areas. This doesn't tackle the poverty or unemployment, and often is simply a way to reclaim the land for development: Europe's worst 18th-century slums, London's Rookeries, are now fashionable Bloomsbury.

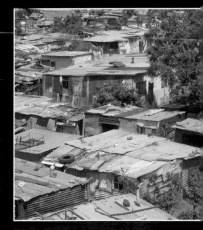

Soweto ▲
Until black South Africans took control of their country in 1994, black families lived outside the main cities in townships. The townships outside Johannesburg became known as Soweto. Many homes were slum dwellings, but there are now permanent homes, hotels and services.

▲ **New York gang land**
When the Five Points district in Manhattan began to sink into a swamp, respectable families moved elsewhere. By the 1830s, the area was a dangerous, disease-filled slum. Irish gangs fought in streets with nicknames like "Murderer's Alley".

Death
of the City

IMAGINE A TOWN SUDDENLY frozen in time, then preserved for 17 centuries. This is no fairy tale: in 79 CE, an Italian volcano, Vesuvius, erupted, entombing the Roman towns of Pompeii and Herculaneum in ash. They remained forgotten until treasure hunters dug them up around 1740.

The tragic death of Pompeii and Herculaneum was dramatic but not unique. A forest swallowed Angkor Wat in Cambodia and the Jamaican town of Port Royal disappeared into the sea.

Today Pompeii is dying again as weather and weeds destroy its priceless Roman buildings

Wild West ghost town ▲
Small towns sprung up like mushrooms in the 19th-century California gold rush – then rotted away almost as fast. A few, such as Bodie, have been preserved. Now a Western ghost town, Bodie once had 65 bars.

Cast of a dog caught in the eruption from Mt Vesuvius

Pompeii and Mt Vesuvius ▼
The eruption of Vesuvius trapped some of Pompeii's 20,000 inhabitants. Ash built up around them, creating moulds of their final moments. Archaeologists excavating the town poured plaster into the moulds, creating tragic, lifelike casts.

Last one out turn off the light

Most dead towns are just abandoned. Their residents gather up their possessions and leave. They may be fleeing wars, disease, drought or starvation. Or perhaps the original reason for the town's existence disappeared. Mining towns, for example, often wither when the ore runs out.

Plague towns ▲
When a plague struck 14th-century Europe, one-third of the continent's people died. Artists drew grim pictures of the dead dancing. The terrified survivors often abandoned their homes, leaving villages to rot.

Many dead cities vanish without a trace. But the few that are preserved intact, such as Machu Picchu, Mesa Verde (see page 21) and Pompeii, provide windows into the past.

◀ Mountain retreat
Disease probably killed the residents of Machu Picchu in Peru in 1550. Its remote location high up in the mountains hid it from the Spanish who conquered the country.

City of vice dies
The Jamaican town of Port Royal had a wicked reputation. The pirates who ruled it spent their booty on booze, gambling and girls. When an earthquake drowned it in the sea in 1692, religious folk claimed that God had punished the city's sinners!

Angkor Wat ▶
The extraordinary, 12th-century Angkor Wat temple was the centrepiece of a gigantic city that's now hidden by forest. Residents probably abandoned the city after the failure of the elaborate system of canals on which their crops depended.

41

Brightening up the City

OVERNIGHT, a brilliant crimson cartoon dog appears on a drab concrete city wall. To the council workers who have to scrub it off in the morning, it's vandalism. But to the painters who stalk the streets at night with paint brushes and spray cans, it's art.

▲ **Oz art**
The Australian city of Melbourne is world famous for street art like this fun dog. The city has hosted a popular and colourful stencil festival every year since 2004.

◀ **Squeezebox sailor**
Visual arts are not the only ones in city streets. Musicians sound better than traffic and provide a chance to hear sounds that are not recorded. Busking like this has launched the careers of many famous performers, including Bob Dylan.

Would You Believe . . . ?

Streets: the new galleries?
British street artist Banksy started his career by poking fun at art galleries: now they buy his work. In 2008, an auctioneer that usually sells Old Master oil paintings sold one of Banksy's stencilled spray paintings for nearly half a million dollars!

◀ **Watch your step**
Street sculpture makes cities more interesting, provides famous landmarks and introduces art to people who would never think of going into an art gallery. This bronze sculpture in Bratislava, Slovakia, additionally celebrates the unseen workers who keep the city running smoothly.

▼ Adding colour to the city scene

Street advertising is ancient – there were painted signs in Pompeii (page 40). Early signs were visible only in daylight. The neon tubes that splash colour all over modern cities first appeared in 1912. Today, advertisers must work hard to catch our attention, as the owners of this crab restaurant in Osaka, Japan, realise!

Graffiti competes for attention with more conventional kinds of street decoration. Advertisers spend millions to make us notice their brand – some in amazing and original ways. And "real" art finds its way into cities as sculpture and murals.

● ● ● ● ● ● ● ● ● ● ● ● ● ● ●

Chicago has the best street art because developers must spend $1 on art for every $75 they spend on building

Street art around the world

Mural artists must think big: they work from scaffolding with *buckets* of paint, not tubes. When their huge artworks are complete, they face problems no gallery artist shares. Tyre dust, rain, air pollution and sunlight can destroy a mural in a decade or less.

▲ Charcoal wall drawing by Jorge Rodriguez-Gerada in Barcelona, Spain

▲ Street art on a house in Olinda, Brazil

◀ Street art in Padangbai, Bali, Indonesia

What Future for the City?

CITIES ARE HERE TO STAY, that's clear. However, today's cities are hungry monsters. They are greedy for space, energy, food and water. Cities cover just one-fiftieth of Earth's dry land. Yet they use three-quarters of its resources.

Would You Believe . . . ?

Farm, town or both?
Tomorrow's cities will feed themselves. The Chinese city of Shanghai already produces all the milk and eggs it needs. In Kolkata, India, some people feast on carp (big goldfish) raised in sewage, and 20,000 farmers grow crops on rubbish dumps.

This can't go on. We need a new kind of city – a city where everything you need is just a walk away; where energy and water are used sparingly; where neighbours know and help each other. What will tomorrow's cities be like?

● ● ● ● ● ● ● ● ● ● ● ● ● ● ● ● ● ● ●

Cars squander precious space and energy: in the future city, all transport will be public transport

City or shanty?
Future cities could have some surprising models – shanty towns. Though they are run-down and unhygienic, shanty towns need few resources, and residents recycle much of what the towns use. They use little space or energy and their streets are made for walking, not driving.

◄ **Picturing the future**
Science fiction movies like *Metropolis* (1927) picture looming high-rise cities of glass, concrete, steel and asphalt. But these materials make cities roast in the summer. In reality, future cities are more likely to feature low-rise buildings kept cool with large areas of grass, water and trees.

Find out More

You can find out lots more about the history of towns from these websites and places to visit.

Websites

Pudding Lane to Pie Corner
www.fireoflondon.org.uk/game
Stay cool and experience the 1666 fire in this game created by the Museum of London.

Splish Splash Splosh
www.pbs.org/wgbh/nova/lostempires/roman/aqueduct.html
Read the Roman water engineer's manual and then decide how to build the aqueduct.

Pompeii the last day
http://dsc.discovery.com/convergence/pompeii/pompeii.html
Discover lots more about Pompeii. Watch Pliny's account of the last day as a web documentary or take the Would You Survive quiz.

Build your own suburb
www.bekonscot.com/virtual_village
Commuter sim, complete with rows of fake 1930s olde-worlde cottages and a train to get to the city.

Head in the clouds
www.pbs.org/wgbh/buildingbig/skyscraper/challenge/index.html
Learn the basics of civil engineering and stop the tall buildings from falling down.

Places to visit

Museum Of London
London Wall
London EC2Y 5HN
Telephone: 0870 444 3851
Website: www.museumoflondon.org.uk/English
The story of London from pre-historic times is told through reconstructed interiors and street scenes, alongside displays of artefacts.

Museum of London Docklands
West India Quay, Canary Wharf
London E14 4AL
Telephone: 0870 444 3857
Website: www.museumindocklands.org.uk/English
From Roman settlement to Docklands regeneration, this 200-year-old warehouse reveals the long history of London as a port, through stories of trade, migration and commerce.

The Real Mary King's Close
2 Warriston's Close, Writers Court
Edinburgh EH1 1PG
Telephone: 08702 430160
Website: www.realmarykingsclose.com
These underground streets of Edinburgh are unchanged since they were entombed in 1753.

Brighton Sewer Tours
Sewer Tours, Communications Department
Southern Water, Southern House, Yeoman Road
Worthing BN13 3NX
Telephone: 01903 272606
Website: www.southernwater.co.uk/homeAndLeisure/daysOut/brightonSewerTours/default.asp
Walk through the sewers from Brighton Pier to Olde Steine Gardens. These award-winning tours of Brighton's sewers run from May to September and must be pre-booked.

Wroxeter Roman City
Wroxeter, near Shrewsbury
Shropshire, SY5 6PH
Telephone: 01743 761330
Website: www.english-heritage.org.uk/wroxeter
Wroxeter was the fourth largest city in Roman Britain. The site museum and audio tour show how the city worked. This English Heritage site was the winner of the Sandford Award for Heritage Education 2008.

JORVIK Viking Centre
Coppergate
York YO1 9WT
Telephone: 01904 534400
Website: www.jorvik-viking-centre.co.uk
Hold your nose as you explore Viking streets, reconstructed as they would have been in 975 CE.

Glossary

Did you read anything you didn't understand? Some of the more complicated and unusual terms used in this book are explained here.

aqueduct
Trough or pipe carrying drinking water.

Arab world
Countries of North Africa and the Middle East, where most people speak Arabic.

archaeologist
Scientist who studies past civilizations through human remains and artefacts.

Aztecs
Native Central-American people who ruled Mexico until it was conquered by Spanish explorers in the 16th century.

biological warfare
Warfare in which weapons kill or injure by spreading deadly germs or poisons.

catacombs
Underground tunnels used instead of graves, or to store the collected bones of the dead.

cutpurse
Thief or pickpocket.

gold rush
Rush of treasure seekers to a newly discovered source of gold.

graffiti
Messages scribbled on walls.

hamlet
Small village.

Mecca
The holy city of the Islamic religion, in Saudi Arabia.

Middle Ages
The period of European history between ancient and modern times: roughly CE 500–1500.

Minoans
People who lived on the Greek island of Crete for over 1,000 years from about 2600 BCE.

moat
Deep, wide ditch surrounding a castle or house, usually filled with water, for protection from attack by enemies.

mud-brick
Brick made of mud mixed with straw and dried in the sun.

mural
Decorative wall-painting.

Neolithic
An ancient time (roughly 10000 to 1000 BCE) when people made polished stone tools.

Olympics
International sports contest, held every four years, imitating an event in ancient Greece.

Ottomans
Turkish rulers who controlled areas around the Black Sea and eastern Mediterranean for 400 years from the 16th century.

plague
A disease that spreads quickly and kills many in a short time.

pollution
Waste from human activity that harms the air, soil or water.

pope
Leader of the Catholic Church.

ramparts
Protected walk-way on top of the walls of a castle or fortress.

revolution
When people rise up to take power from a government.

skyscraper
Very tall building, especially in cities in the USA.

smog
Fog made worse by smoke or other *pollution* in the air.

trade route
Route that merchants follow, transporting their goods.

tsunami
Giant wave, usually caused by an earthquake or *volcano*.

vandalism
Pointless destruction of valuable things or those in a public place.

volcano
Place where Earth's liquid core breaks through gaps in the crust.

wholesale market
Market for shopkeepers, rather than for the public.

Index

Picture credits

The publisher would like to thank the following for their kind permission to reproduce their photographs:

Position key: c=centre; b=bottom; left=left; r=right; t=top

4bc: akg-images; 5c: Heritage Image Partnership; 5bc: iStockphoto; 6bc: iStockphoto; 9cr: Roger Wood/Corbis; 10bc: Heritage Image Partnership; 13bc: Historical Pictures Archive/Corbis; 14bc: Bildarchiv Monheim GmbH/Alamy; 14tl: Robert Kerton/iStockphoto; 15tc: Muzzi Fabio/Corbis Sygma; 16tr: North Wind Picture Archives/Alamy; 17bc: Jon Arnold Images Ltd/Alamy; 18bc: Mary Evans Picture Library/Alamy; 18tr: Paul Kingsley/Alamy; 19c: Ricardo Beliel/BrazilPhoto/Alamy; 20bc: Simon Podgoresk/iStockphoto; 21cl: Alain Couillaud/iStockphoto; 22cl: The Print Collector/Alamy; 23bc: Heritage Image Partnership; 23c: iStockphoto; 24cl: Mary Evans Picture Library; 25cr: The Print Collector/Alamy; 25bl: Mike Liu/iStockphoto; 25c: iStockphoto; 26bc: iStockphoto; 26cr: RKO/

The Kobal Collection; 27bl: Bettmann/Corbis; 27tr: iStockphoto; 28cl: H. Armstrong Roberts/ClassicStock/Corbis; 28tr: Brandon Laufenberg/iStockphoto; 29bl: Mary Evans Picture Library/Alamy; 29tr: Mary Evans Picture Library; 30bl: View Stock/Alamy; 30cl: North Wind Picture Archives/Alamy; 30tr: Heritage Image Partnership; 30c: Ronald Bloom/iStockphoto; 31bc: Tengku Mohd Yusof/Alamy; 31tr: iStockphoto; 32bl: iStockphoto; 33cr: Yang Liu/Corbis; 33tr: Heritage Image Partnership; 33bl: Jim Ptuitt/iStockphoto; 33cl: Mary Evans Picture Library; 34cr: Gary Doak/Alamy; 34tl: iStockphoto/Fernig; 34bl: Steve Duncan; 35bc: Yann Arthus-Bertard/Corbis; 36cr: Oleg Kozlov/iStockphoto; 36bc: iDtockphoto; 37bc: Paolo Gallo/Alamy; 37cr: Swim Ink 2,LLC/Corbis; 37tc: Oleg Kozlov/iStockphoto; 37tr: Kirill Zdotov/iStockphoto; 37tl: Oleg Kozlov/iStockphoto; 38bc: Liba Taylor/Corbis; 39bc: Geoffery Clements/Corbis; 39tc: Richard Goerg/iStockphoto; 40bc: Arialdo Rescigno/iStockphoto; 40tr: John Sullivan; 41br: Serdar Yaggi/iStockphoto; 42cr: Chris Willson/Alamy; 42cl: Luis Sandoval/iStockphoto; 42bc: Stefan Muran/iStockphoto; 42tl: Richard Platt; 43cr: Shawn Liposki; 43cr: Bjorn Christian Torrissen; 43cr: Davenbelle; 44cl: UFS/The Kobal Collection